italian
al dente

SILVERDALE BOOKS

Published in 2001 by Silverdale Books
An Imprint of Bookmart Ltd.
Registered Number 2372865
Trading as Bookmart Limited
Desford Road
Enderby
Leicester
LE9 5AD
Copyright (c) Trident Press International 2001

Italian Al Dente
Compiled by: R&R Publications Marketing Pty. Ltd.
Creative Director: Paul Sims
Production Manager: Anthony Carroll
Food Photography: Warren Webb
Food Stylists: Stephane Souvlis, Janet Lodge,
Di Kirby
Recipe Development: Ellen Argyriou,
Sheryle Eastwood, Kim Freedman,
Lucy Kelly, Donna Hay
Proof Reader: Andrea Hazell-Tarttelin

Includes Index
ISBN 1 85605 651 1
EAN 9781856056519

First Edition Printed February 2001
Computer Typeset in Humanist 521
& Times New Roman

Printed in China

Italian glossary

When browsing through a book about Italian food or working through a menu or recipe, a term sometimes crops up which is unfamiliar unclear. This list of words and phrases commonly used around an Italian kitchen may help make your reading more rewarding and enjoyable.

Affumicato	Smoked
Agio e ogio	Garlic and oil, as a dressing
Al dente	To the tooth, a texture with some bite to it
Al forno/alla fornaia	In the oven; baked or roasted
Antipasto	The very first course of a meal; starter
Arrosto	Roasted, baked
Asciutto	Dry, as in pasta asciutto
Bollito	Boiled, particularly boiled meat
Cacciatora	Hunter's style
Caldo	Hot
Casalinga	Homemade
Condito	Dressed, as in a salad
Contorno	Vegetable dish, garnish
Cotto	Cooked
Crudo	Raw, uncooked
Cucina	Kitchen
Diavola	Devilled, or with a spicy sauce
Dolce	Sweets, dessert
Farcito	Stuffed
Fritto misto	Mixed fry
Freddo	Cold
Fresco	Fresh, cool
Fritto	Fried
Grasso	Fat
Integrale	Wholemeal
Il primo	The meal course between antipasto and the main course, consisting of soup, pasta, risotto or polenta
Il secondo	The main course of a meal
Magro	Thin, lean
Paglia e fieno	Straw and hay, meaning green and white
Pelato	Peeled
Petto	Breast, e.g. breast of chicken
Piatto	Plate
Ragu	Rich meat sauce
Ripieno	Stuffed
Rotolo	Roll, as in a Swiss roll
Rustico	Rustic
Saor	Soused, as with fish
Secco	Dry
Soffritto	A mixture of chopped vegetables fried in butter or oil and used as a flavour base for soups, sauces and stews
Sugo	Sauce, usually for pasta
Tavola	Table
Tritato	Minced, finely chopped
Verde	Green
Verdure	Vegetables

cheese

Gorgonzola, mascarpone, Parmesan, pecorino – the list of Italy's splendid cheeses is virtually endless. Different regions have developed unique cheese styles over the centuries, and whether you're cooking with an Italian cheese, adding one to a cooked dish, or assembling a cheese platter, you're dealing with some of the world's best.

The cheeses of Italy originated in the dairies and kitchens of farmers. Now, each region has at least one cheese that is characteristic of it, and this is reflected in that region's cooking. It would be difficult to create authentic Italian dishes without having the appropriate cheese available and we are lucky that most cheese counters offer a range of both imported and locally made cheeses to choose from. Price is not always an indication of which is best, so it is a good idea to taste-test before buying.

Bel Paese

Meaning 'beautiful country', Bel Paese is a commercial variation of a mild, semi-soft, creamy cheese made from cow's milk. Originating from the Lombardy region, it melts easily and is perfect for cooking. Bel Paese can be used in place of mozzarella and fontina.

Caciocavallo

Harking from southern Italy and Sicily it is made from cow's milk and is sometimes mixed with goat's milk. The name means 'cheese on horseback', which refers to the way the cheeses are strung together in pairs and hung to mature over poles, as if astride a horse. When fresh, it is soft and sweet and eaten as a table cheese. When aged, it becomes spicy and tangy and should be used for grating. If unavailable, use provolone which is the more widely known member of the same family of cheeses.

Dolcelatte

One of the Gorgonzola cheeses, its name means 'sweet milk'.

Fontina

A semi-hard cow's milk cheese with a sweet and nutty flavour. Although classified as a table cheese, it is most commonly used in fonduta, a traditional dish from the region of Piemont. If fontina is unavailable, use gruyère for a fondue, or Bel Paese or matured mozzarella for other dishes.

Gorgonzola

Made from cow's milk, it has a soft, creamy texture and a buttery flavour. Its characteristic blue mould is produced by introducing a harmless penicillin bacteria to the cheese. There are several kinds of Gorgonzola, with Dolcelatte being the best known. Meaning 'sweet milk', it is the creamiest and sweetest variety. Dolce verde is more piquant and is stronger in flavour and smell. You can use any other creamy, mild blue-vein cheese, or blend some cream with a sharper, crumbly blue-vein in place of Gorgonzola.

Grana

A collective name used to describe matured, hard cheeses from northern and central Italy, these cheeses have a close grain ideal for grating. Parmesan and grana padano are the most well-known in this group of cheeses. Grana padano is made from cow's milk from areas outside those designated for reggiano production. Because of a shorter maturing time it is less flavoursome and moister than Parmesan. Wherever possible, grana cheeses should be bought in a piece to be freshly grated as required.

Mascarpone

A fresh cheese made from cream, Mascarpone is unsalted, buttery and rich with a fat content of 90 percent. It is used mostly as a dessert, either alone or as an ingredient. If it is unavailable, mix one part thick sour cream to three parts thickened (double) cream or beat 250g/8oz ricotta cheese with 250mL/8fl oz pure (single) cream until smooth and thick.

wine

Italian wines:

The climate and soil of Italy are perfect for wine production and every region produces wine. In fact, Italy produces more wine than any other country in the world.

Aperitifs:

Campari

This is a strong alcohol which is usually served with soda water.

Vermouth

A fortified wine. The French also have a vermouth but you will find that the Italian one is much sweeter.

White Wines:

Frascati

Ideal for serving with fish and chicken. It is a light, dry straw-coloured wine that ranges from dry to sweet. The sweet frascati is known as Canellino and makes a good accompaniment to beans and gnocchi. Dry frascati is the best known of this group of wines.

Verdicchio

A young, light, fresh, fruity semi-dry wine.

Red Wines:

Lambrusco

A light, dry, slightly sparkling wine, good to serve with meat meals.

Barbera

This robust red wine complements the full flavour of Italian food.

Chianti

Available as either red or white wine. As a young wine, chianti is wonderfully fragrant and fruity; as it ages it becomes even better. This is the wine that is found in the straw-covered bottles so often associated with Italy.

Dessert Wines:

Marsala

This fortified, full-flavoured sweet wine is named after a town on the island of Sicily. It is used mainly for cooking and dessert, however some varieties are also drunk as aperitifs.

Vin Santo

A dessert wine from Tuscany. It is made from grapes that are dried in the shade for several months. They are then pressed and the wine aged for four to five years in small oak casks. The casks are stored under the roof, thereby exposing the wine to variations in temperature, which adds to the unique flavour.

Sparkling Wines:

Asti Spumanti

The best known sweet Italian sparkling wine that makes a perfect finish to a meal. It is made in vast quantities and exported all over the world.

Liqueurs:

Galliano

A rich yellow liqueur flavoured with herbs.

Sambuca

A clear anise-flavoured liqueur.

Amaretto

A rich toffee-coloured liqueur that tastes of almonds.

Frangelico

A delicious liqueur made from hazelnuts, berries, almonds, orange flowers and cinnamon.

mixed bean soup

soups
&
starters

From classic favourites like Minestrone

to more luxurious dishes like Butterflied Prawns with Garlic, Chilli and Parsley, you are sure to be inspired to try the delicious soup and starter ideas on the following pages.

8

roasted
eggplant soup

Photograph opposite

ingredients

I kg/2 lb eggplant (aubergines), halved
4 red capsicums (peppers), halved
I teaspoon olive oil
2 cloves garlic, crushed
4 tomatoes, peeled and chopped
3 cups/750mL/I¼ pt vegetable stock
2 teaspoons crushed black peppercorns

roasted eggplant soup

Method:

1 Place eggplant (aubergines) and red capsicums (peppers), skin side up under a preheated hot grill and cook for 10 minutes or until flesh is soft and skins are blackened. Peel away blackened skin and roughly chop flesh.

2 Heat oil in a large saucepan over a medium heat. Add garlic and tomatoes and cook, stirring, for 2 minutes. Add eggplant (aubergines), red peppers, stock and black pepper, bring to simmer and leave for 4 minutes. Remove pan from heat and set aside to cool slightly.

3 Place vegetables and stock in batches in food processor or blender and process until smooth. Return mixture to a clean pan, bring to simmer over a medium heat and simmer for 3-5 minutes or until heated through.

Note: This soup can be made the day before and reheated when required.

Serves 6

minestrone

Method:

1 Heat butter and add garlic, onion, bacon and bones. Sauté 4-5 minutes.
2 Add all other ingredients except pasta and bring to the boil. Allow to simmer covered for approximately 90 minutes.
3 Remove and discard bacon bones.
4 Stir in both pastas and cook until al dente.
   Note: To serve, sprinkle with a generous helping of Parmesan and a good crusty loaf of your favourite bread.

Serves 4

ingredients

2 tablespoons/60g/2oz butter
2 cloves garlic, crushed
2 small onions, finely chopped
4 rashers bacon, chopped
250g/8oz bacon bones
150g/4½oz red kidney beans
100g/3½oz haricot beans, soaked overnight
½ small cabbage, roughly chopped
100g/3½oz spinach, washed and chopped
3 medium-sized potatoes, peeled and chopped
2 medium-sized carrots, peeled and diced
150g/4½oz fresh (or frozen) peas, shelled
1 stalk celery, chopped
2 tablespoons parsley, finely chopped
2 litres/3½pt chicken stock
salt to taste
100g/3½oz tomato and cheese tortellini
50g/2oz pasta of your choice
fresh Parmesan cheese

Oven temperature 200°C, 400°F, Gas 6

tomato
and basil bruschetta

Method:
1 Combine oil and garlic. Brush bread slices liberally with oil mixture and place on an oiled baking tray. Bake for 10 minutes or until bread is golden. Set aside to cool.
2 Place tomatoes, basil or parsley and black pepper to taste in a bowl and mix to combine. Just prior to serving, top toasted bread slices with tomato mixture.
Note: For a light meal, top bruschetta with a little grated Parmesan or mozzarella cheese and grill until cheese melts. Serve with a salad.

Serves 6

ingredients

¹/₂ cup/125mL/4fl oz olive oil
2 cloves garlic, crushed
1 French bread stick, sliced diagonally
3 tomatoes, finely chopped
3 tablespoons chopped fresh basil or parsley
freshly ground black pepper

tuna and beans

Method:
1. Place tuna, beans and onion in a bowl and mix gently so that tuna remains in chunks.
2. Place oil, vinegar, garlic and mustard in a screwtop jar and shake well to combine.
3. Pour dressing over tuna mixture and toss gently. Stand at room temperature for 1 hour. Sprinkle with parsley and serve.

Serves 6

ingredients

375g/12oz can tuna in oil, drained
440g/14oz can red kidney beans, drained
1/2 red onion, diced
60mL/2fl oz olive oil
1 tablespoon wine vinegar
1 small clove garlic, crushed
1 teaspoon French mustard
chopped fresh parsley to serve

capsicums
(peppers) roasted in garlic

Method:
1. Preheat oven to 180°C/350°F/Gas 4. Place red capsicum (pepper) in a bowl. Combine oil, garlic, red chilli and oregano, pour over capsicum and toss to coat.
2. Layer capsicum (pepper), skin side up, in a baking dish, cover with aluminium foil and bake for 30 minutes. Uncover and bake for 20-30 minutes longer or until capsicum (pepper) blackens slightly.

Note: When available, use a mixture of red, green and yellow capsicum (peppers). Store, covered with olive oil, in a clean glass jar for up to 3 weeks. The capsicums (peppers) taste best served at room temperature.

Serves 6

ingredients

3 red capsicums (peppers), cut lengthwise into eighths
1 1/2 tablespoons olive oil
5 cloves garlic, finely chopped
1 fresh red chilli, cut into slivers
1/2 teaspoon dried oregano

Oven temperature 180°C, 350°F, Gas 4

14

eggplant
antipasto

Method:

1 *Sprinkle eggplant (aubergine) with salt and stand for 15-20 minutes. Rinse under cold water and pat dry with absorbent paper.*

2 *Brush eggplant (aubergine) lightly with olive oil. Place under a preheated grill for 4-5 minutes each side or until cooked through.*

3 *Divide eggplant (aubergine) into four portions of three or four slices, overlapping in a shallow ovenproof dish. Top with mozzarella and grill for 4-5 minutes or until cheese melts.*

4 *Transfer eggplant (aubergine) to four plates. Top with capers and serve with an arrangement of gherkins, tomatoes, ham, bread, lettuce and chutney.*

Serves 4

ingredients

2 eggplant(aubergine), cut into
2 cm/1in slices
salt
olive oil
150g sliced mozzarella cheese
1 tablespoon capers
2 gerkins, sliced lenghtwise
2 tomatoes, sliced
12 slices leg ham or prosciutto, rolled
4 slices rye or wholemeal bread
4 lettuce leaves
4 tablespoons chutney or relish

butterflied
prawns with garlic, chilli and parsley

Method:

1 *Cut prawns down the back and remove vein.*
2 *Combine oil, lemon juice, garlic, chilli and parsley in a bowl. Add prawns, mix well, and leave to marinate for 2-3 hours.*
3 *Heat oil in a large pan, coat prawns with flour, and cook quickly in oil for 2-3 minutes. Drain on absorbent paper.*
4 *Serve with lemon wedges and parsley.*

Serves 4

ingredients

**1kg/2¼ lb (approx. 20) green prawns,
heads and shells removed,
tails left on
2 tablespoons olive oil
1 tablespoon lemon juice
2 cloves garlic, crushed
2 red chillies, seeded
and finely chopped
2 tablespoons parsley, chopped
½ cup/60g/2oz flour
oil (for frying)
lemon (to garnish)**

mixed
bean soup

Photograph page 9

ingredients

90g/3oz dried red kidney beans
90g/3oz dried cannellini beans
2 tablespoons olive oil
60g/2oz bacon, chopped
1 onion, chopped
1 clove garlic, crushed
3 stalks celery, sliced
2 carrots, chopped
2 potatoes, chopped
6 cups/1¹/₂ litres/2¹/₂pt chicken or
vegetable stock
440g/14oz canned tomatoes,
undrained and mashed
¹/₄ cabbage, finely shredded
60g/2oz small pasta shapes or rice
1 teaspoon dried mixed herbs
freshly ground black pepper
grated Parmesan cheese

Method:

1 *Place red kidney and cannellini beans in a bowl. Cover with cold water and set aside to soak overnight. Drain.*
2 *Heat oil in a saucepan over a medium heat, add bacon, onion and garlic and cook, stirring, for 5 minutes or until onion is tender. Add celery, carrots and potatoes and cook for 1 minute longer.*
3 *Stir in stock, tomatoes, cabbage, pasta or rice, red kidney and cannellini beans, herbs and black pepper to taste and bring to the boil. Boil for 10 minutes, then reduce heat and simmer, stirring occasionally, for 1 hour or until beans are tender. Sprinkle with Parmesan cheese and serve.*

Note: *This minestrone-style soup is delicious served with hot crusty bread.*
Extra vegetables of your choice may be added – it is a good way to use up odds and ends.

Serves 4

fresh
basil carpaccio

Method:

1 *To make dressing, place basil, oil, lemon juice, capers and garlic in a bowl. Mix well to combine.*

2 *Arrange beef slices on a serving plate and season with black pepper. Pour dressing over and sprinkle with onion. Cover and marinate for 10 minutes.*

Serves 4

ingredients

500g/1lb eye fillet, very thinly sliced
1 onion, finely sliced
freshly ground black pepper
<u>Basil Dressing</u>
10 fresh basil leaves, chopped
4 tablespoons olive oil
3 tablespoons lemon juice
2 tablespoons capers, chopped
2 cloves garlic, finely chopped

chargrilled
vegetables with pesto

Method:

1 Prepare vegetables for grilling.
2 Grease and heat a chargrill pan. Brush vegetable slices with a little olive oil and chargrill until golden brown and vegetables are cooked.
3 Serve with pesto or basil aïoli.

Serves 4

ingredients

1 capsicum (pepper), cut into pieces
1 eggplant (aubergine), cut into slices
2 red onions, quartered
2 zucchini/courgette, sliced lengthwise
1 small sweet potato, thinly sliced
olive oil
pesto of choice

spinach and ricotta cannelloni

pasta
&
rice

Few things are more delicious than a

creamy risotto or a dish of gnocchi.
The best results require a little patience,
but they are worth every minute. When you
see these dishes, you'll understand why the
Italians love them so.

spaghetti
with meatballs

Photograph opposite

spaghetti with meatballs

ingredients

500g/1 lb lean minced beef
2 tablespoons chopped fresh parsley
60g/2oz salami, very finely chopped
60g/2oz grated Parmesan cheese
3 tablespoons tomato purée
1 egg, beaten
15g/¹/₂oz butter
1 onion, very finely chopped
2 teaspoons dried basil
1 teaspoon dried oregano
440g/14oz can tomatoes, chopped
125mL/4fl oz beef stock
125mL/4fl oz white wine
1 teaspoon caster sugar
250g/8oz spaghetti

Method:

1 *Combine beef, parsley, salami, Parmesan cheese and 1 tablespoon tomato purée in a bowl, mix in enough egg to bind. Form mixture into small balls, cook in a nonstick frying pan for 10-12 minutes until cooked, then set aside.*

2 *Melt butter in a large frying pan over moderate heat. Add onion, basil and oregano and cook for 2 minutes. Stir in tomatoes, remaining tomato purée, beef stock, wine and sugar. Simmer mixture for 30 minutes, stirring occasionally, until thick.*

3 *Cook spaghetti in boiling salted water until just tender, drain. Stir meatballs into the tomato sauce, warm through, stirring occasionally. Serve on a bed of spaghetti.*

Kitchen Tip: *To cut down on preparation time make the meatballs in advance and freeze them in the tomato sauce in a covered container for up to 3 months. Simply reheat over a gentle heat when required and serve with spaghetti.*

Serves 4

23

saffron
and chicken risotto

Method:

1 Place stock and wine in a saucepan and bring to the boil over a medium heat. Reduce heat and keep warm.

2 Heat oil in a saucepan over a medium heat, add chicken and cook, stirring, for 5 minutes or until chicken is tender. Remove chicken from pan and set aside.

3 Add butter and leeks to same pan and cook over a low heat, stirring, for 8 minutes or until leeks are golden and caramelised.

4 Add rice and saffron to pan and cook over a medium heat, stirring constantly, for 3 minutes or until rice becomes translucent. Pour 1 cup/250 mL/8 fl oz hot stock mixture into rice mixture and cook, stirring constantly, until liquid is absorbed. Continue cooking in this way until all the stock is used and rice is tender.

5 Stir chicken, Parmesan cheese and black pepper to taste into rice mixture and cook for 2 minutes longer. Serve immediately.

ingredients

4 cups/1 litre/1³/₄pt vegetable stock
1 cup/250mL/8fl oz dry white wine
1 tablespoon vegetable oil
2 boneless chicken breast fillets, sliced
45g/¹/₂oz butter
3 leeks, sliced
2 cups/440g/14oz arborio or risotto rice
pinch saffron threads
60g/2oz grated Parmesan cheese
freshly ground black pepper

Note: *Arborio rice is traditionally used for making risottos, as it absorbs liquid without becoming soft. If arborio rice is unavailable, substitute with any short grain rice. A risotto made in the traditional way, where liquid is added a little at a time as the rice cooks, will take 20-30 minutes to cook.*

Serves 4

chicken
livers and mushrooms on spaghetti

Method:

1 To make tomato sauce, heat oil and butter in a frypan, and cook onion until soft. Add garlic and mushrooms and cook for 2-3 minutes longer. Combine tomatoes and sugar and add to mushrooms. Cook over a low heat for 10 minutes. Stir in stock and simmer for 30 minutes longer or until sauce reduces and thickens. Season to taste with black pepper.

2 To make chicken liver sauce, melt butter in a saucepan and cook chicken livers and thyme over a medium heat until brown. Increase heat, stir in Marsala and cook for 1-2 minutes. Stir in parsley.

3 Cook spaghetti in boiling water in a large saucepan until al dente. Drain and fold through oil.

4 Arrange half spaghetti on a warm serving platter, top with half chicken liver mixture, then half Tomato Sauce. Sprinkle over half Parmesan cheese, then repeat layers. Serve immediately.

Note: This recipe is a variation of a sauce created for the great singer Caruso.

Serves 4

ingredients

500 g/1 lb fresh spaghetti, or
400g/13oz dried spaghetti
1 tablespoon vegetable oil
90g/3oz grated fresh Parmesan cheese
<u>Tomato sauce</u>
1 tablespoon vegetable oil
30g/1oz butter
1 onion, finely diced
2 cloves garlic, crushed
12 small button mushrooms, halved
440g/14oz canned Italian peeled tomatoes,
undrained and mashed
1 teaspoon sugar
300mL/9 1/2fl oz chicken stock
ground black pepper
<u>Chicken liver sauce</u>
30g/1oz butter
250g/8oz chicken livers, trimmed and sliced
1 teaspoon finely chopped fresh thyme,
or 1/4 teaspoon dried thyme
90mL/3fl oz Marsala
1 tablespoon finely chopped fresh parsley

rice
with mozzarella and herbs

Method:

1 Place water in a large saucepan and bring to the boil. Add rice and cook, covered, for 15-20 minutes or until the rice is just tender. Stir occasionally during cooking to prevent sticking.

2 Drain, then return rice to same pan. Stir in butter and chopped herbs then fold through mozzarella and Parmesan cheeses and season to taste with black pepper. Transfer to a warm serving dish and serve immediately.

Note: Much simpler than a risotto, this dish relies on the quality of the fresh herbs and mozzarella used.

Serves 4

ingredients

4 litres/7pt water
315g/10oz arborio rice
90g/3oz butter, cut into small pieces
2 tablespoons fresh mixed herbs, chopped
250g/8oz grated mozzarella cheese
60g/2oz grated fresh Parmesan cheese
freshly ground black pepper

seafood
lasagne

Method:

1 *Preheat oven to 180°C/350°F/Gas 4. Heat the oil in a large frying pan, add the leek and cook until tender. Stir in the tomatoes and tomato purée. Cook until mixture boils then simmer uncovered until sauce is slightly thickened. Stir in the prawn and fish pieces, cover and cook over low heat for about 5 minutes.*

2 *Cook the lasagne in a saucepan of boiling water until al dente. Place lasagne in a large bowl of cool water until ready to use.*

3 *Spoon one third of the sauce into the bottom of a 5cm/2in-deep casserole dish. Drain lasagne sheets and arrange a single layer over the seafood sauce. Spoon another third of the sauce over the lasagne, and top with another layer of lasagne.*

4 *Spread the remaining third of sauce over lasagne and top with mozzarella cheese. Bake in oven for 40 minutes.*

Serves 4

ingredients

2 tablespoons olive oil
1 leek, white part only, finely chopped
440g/14oz chopped canned tomatoes
2 tablespoons tomato purée
500g/1 lb uncooked prawns, shelled and deveined, cut into small pieces
250g/8oz boneless white fish fillets, cut into small pieces
15 sheets spinach lasagne
125g/4oz mozzarella cheese, thinly sliced

Oven temperature 180°C, 350°F, Gas 4

27

linguine
with prawns and scallops in a roasted tomato sauce

Photograph opposite

linguine with prawns and scallops in a roasted tomato sauce

ingredients

400g/14oz linguine
1kg/2¹/₂ lb tomatoes
salt and pepper
80mL/3oz olive oil
200g/7oz scallops
200g/7oz green prawns, peeled
150g calamari, cut into rings
200g/7oz firm white fish pieces
3 garlic cloves, crushed
2 brown onions, diced
1 tablespoon tomato paste (optional)
80mL/3oz water
¹/₃ cup/20g/²/₃oz parsley, chopped
Parmesan cheese

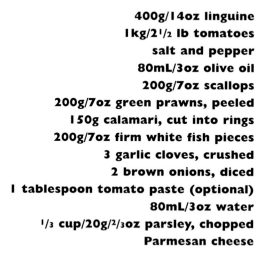

Method:

1 Cook the linguine in salted boiling water until al dente and set aside.

2 To roast the tomatoes: preheat the oven to 180°C/350°F/Gas 4. Cut the tomatoes in half and place on a baking tray. Drizzle with a little olive oil, sprinkle with a little salt and pepper, and roast in the oven for 20-25 minutes until tomatoes are well roasted.

3 Place roasted tomatoes in a food processor and process for a few seconds, but do not over-process. (The mixture should still have texture.)

4 Heat half the oil in a pan. Sauté the scallops and the prawns for 2 minutes until just cooked, and remove from the pan. Add the calamari and cook for 2 minutes, before removing from the pan. Adding a little more oil if needed, sauté the fish for a few minutes until just cooked, and remove from the pan.

5 Heat the remaining oil, and sauté the garlic and onion for a few minutes until cooked. Add the tomato mixture, tomato paste and water, and simmer (for 10 minutes). Carefully add the seafood to the sauce, season with salt and pepper, and mix through the chopped parsley.

6 Serve with the linguine and Parmesan cheese.
Serves 4

mixed mushroom
risotto

Method:

1 In a pan, heat the butter, add the mushrooms, and cook for a few minutes. Remove from the heat and set aside.

2 Heat the oil in a large heavy-based saucepan, add the garlic and leek, and cook for 5-6 minutes until cooked. Meanwhile, place stock in a saucepan and simmer gently.

3 Add the rice and stir for 1 minute, coating the rice in oil. Add the white wine, and cook until liquid is absorbed. Start adding the stock a ladle at a time, stirring continuously until liquid has been absorbed. Continue adding stock a ladle at a time until stock is used and rice is cooked.

4 Stir in mushrooms, lemon rind, cheeses and parsley and serve immediately.

ingredients

2 tablespoons butter
500g/1 lb mixed mushrooms (oyster, shiitake, flat, enoki, Swiss), sliced
40mL/1 1/2fl oz olive oil
2 cloves garlic, minced
1 leek, finely sliced
1 litre/1 3/4pt chicken stock
2 cups arborio rice
1/2 cup/120mL/4fl oz white wine
rind of 1 lemon, finely grated
1/2 cup/60g/2oz each pecorino and Parmesan cheese, grated
2 tablespoons parsley, chopped

Serves 6-8

spinach,
green pea & ricotta gnocchi

Method:

1 Steam or microwave spinach until tender. Drain and squeeze to remove excess liquid. Set aside.

2 Boil, steam or microwave peas until tender. Drain and combine with spinach. Chop mixture finely.

3 Place spinach mixture and ricotta in a saucepan. Season to taste with black pepper and nutmeg. Add 15g/¹/₂oz butter and cook over a very low heat, stirring frequently until butter melts and all excess liquid evaporates. Remove from heat. Beat in eggs, then add the breadcrumbs, flour and half the Parmesan cheese. The mixture should be firm enough to hold its shape, but soft enough to create a light-textured gnocchi.

4 Using well-floured hands, take heaped spoons of mixture and roll lightly into small oval balls. Bring a large saucepan of water to the boil, then reduce heat. Drop gnocchi in a few at a time and cook for 4-5 minutes or until they rise to the surface. Remove from pan and drain. Cover and keep warm.

5 Melt remaining butter in a saucepan and cook until lightly browned. Pour butter over gnocchi, sprinkle with remaining Parmesan cheese and serve.

Serves 4

ingredients

220g/7oz fresh spinach leaves, or 200g/6¹/₂oz frozen spinach, thawed and drained
220g/7oz shelled fresh or frozen green peas
220g/7oz ricotta cheese, drained
freshly ground black pepper
ground nutmeg
60g/2oz butter
2 eggs, lightly beaten
3 tablespoons dried breadcrumbs
5 tablespoons plain flour
90g/3oz fresh Parmesan cheese, grated

spinach
and ricotta cannelloni

Photograph page 21

Method:

1 To make filling, place spinach and water in a saucepan, cover with a tight fitting lid and cook over a medium heat, shaking pan occasionally, for 4-5 minutes or until spinach wilts. Drain well, squeezing out excess water and set aside to cool.

2 Finely chop spinach and place in a bowl. Add ricotta cheese, Parmesan cheese, egg, nutmeg and black pepper to taste and mix to combine. Spoon mixture into cannelloni tubes and arrange tubes side-by-side in a lightly greased ovenproof dish.

3 Combine tomatoes and garlic in a bowl and spoon over cannelloni. Sprinkle with mozzarella cheese and Parmesan cheese and bake for 30-35 minutes or until cannelloni is tender and top is golden.

Note: Cottage cheese may be used in place of the ricotta cheese if you wish. If using cottage cheese, push through a sieve to achieve a smoother texture. Serve cannelloni with an Italian salad and herb or garlic bread.

Serves 4

ingredients

250g/8oz instant (no precooking required) cannelloni tubes
440g/14oz canned tomatoes, drained and chopped
1 clove garlic, crushed
125g/4oz grated mozzarella cheese
2 tablespoons grated Parmesan cheese
<u>Spinach filling</u>
1/2 bunch/250g/8oz English spinach, shredded
1/2 cup/125mL/4fl oz water
250g/8oz ricotta cheese, drained
2 tablespoons grated Parmesan cheese
1 egg, beaten
1/4 teaspoon ground nutmeg
freshly ground black pepper

Oven temperature 180°C, 350°F, Gas 4

pappardelle
with peas and bacon

Method:

1 Melt butter in a large frypan and cook onion, garlic and chilli for 6-8 minutes. Add bacon and cook for 5 minutes longer. Stir in peas, mint and 2 teaspoons parsley. Season to taste with black pepper. Set aside and keep warm.

2 Cook pappardelle in boiling water in a large saucepan until al dente. Drain, then add to pea mixture, toss lightly to coat and remove from heat. Combine eggs, cream, pecorino and remaining parsley and stir into pasta mixture. Serve as soon as eggs begin to set and cling to pasta- this will take only a few seconds. The sauce should be slightly runny.

Serves 4

ingredients

60g/2 oz butter
I onion, sliced
I clove garlic, crushed
pinch chilli flakes, or to taste
3 bacon rashers, chopped
90g/3 oz shelled peas, blanched
I teaspoon mint, finely chopped
I tablespoon fresh parsley, finely chopped
freshly ground black pepper
500g/I lb fresh pappardelle
2 eggs, lightly beaten
90 mL/3fl oz cream (single)
I tablespoon pecorino cheese, grated

poultry

chicken with ricotta, rocket &
roasted red capsicum (peppers)

Today, alongside the standard

commercially raised poultry, the eager
Italian cook can also find quails and
spatchcock that have been commercially
grown. However, for the Italian who enjoys
poultry, nothing beats the taste of wildlife.

chicken
with anchovy sauce

Photograph opposite

ingredients

1¹/₂kg/3 lb chicken, jointed
freshly ground black pepper
1¹/₂ tablespoons olive oil
1 small onion, finely chopped
1 clove garlic, finely chopped
125mL/4fl oz dry white wine
1¹/₂ tablespoons white wine vinegar
125 mL/4fl oz chicken stock
¹/₂ teaspoon dried oregano
1 bay leaf
1 tablespoon slivered black olives
3 flat anchovy fillets, rinsed in cold water,
dried and chopped
2 tablespoons chopped parsley

chicken with anchovy sauce

Method:
1 Wash chicken under cold running water, then pat dry with absorbent kitchen paper. Season to taste with black pepper.
2 Heat oil in a heavy-based frypan and cook chicken a few pieces at a time, until brown on both sides. Remove from pan and set aside. Drain off pan juices and discard.
3 Add onion and garlic to pan and cook, stirring constantly, for 5 minutes or until lightly browned. Stir in wine and vinegar, bring to the boil and simmer until reduced to 3 tablespoons.

4 Pour in chicken stock and boil stirring constantly, for 2 minutes. Return chicken to the pan, add oregano and bay leaf. Bring to the boil, cover and simmer for 30 minutes or until tender.
5 Remove chicken pieces from pan and set aside to keep warm. Remove and discard bay leaf. Bring stock to the boil and boil until slightly thickened. Stir in olives, anchovies and parsley and cook for 1 minute longer, then spoon over chicken.

Serves 4

spatchcock
with ricotta and herbs

Method:

1 To make stuffing, place all ingredients in a bowl and mix well. Divide into four portions. Gently ease skin from breast of each bird and fill pocket with stuffing.

2 Brush birds with oil and top with a sprig of rosemary and a sprinkle of black pepper. Place on a roasting rack in a baking dish and cook at 220°C/425°F/Gas 7 for 30 minutes. Reduce heat to 180°C/350°F/Gas 4 and cook, basting with pan juices, for 20 minutes longer or until birds are tender.

3 Remove birds and set aside to keep warm. Place baking dish over a hot plate and bring juices to the boil, pour over birds and serve.

Serves 4

ingredients

4 x 500g/1 lb spatchcocks, cleaned and dried
2 tablespoons olive oil
4 fresh rosemary sprigs
Freshly ground black pepper
<u>Stuffing</u>
155g/5oz ricotta cheese
60g/2oz finely grated fontina cheese
60g/2oz gorgonzola cheese, crumbled
4 slices mortadella, finely chopped
2 tablespoons fresh parsley, finely chopped
1 tablespoon fresh marjoram, finely chopped
1 tablespoon fresh sage, finely chopped
30g/1oz butter, melted

Oven temperature 180°C, 350°F, Gas 4

chicken
with ricotta, rocket & roasted red capsicum (peppers)

Method:

1 Preheat the oven to 200°C/400°C/Gas 6.
2 Combine ricotta, rocket, pine nuts, capsicum (pepper), and pepper & salt in a small bowl and mix together until smooth.
3 Place 1-2 tablespoons of ricotta mixture under the skin of each chicken breast. Lightly grease a baking dish. Place the chicken breasts in the dish, sprinkle with pepper and salt, place 1 teaspoon butter on each breast, pour stock around the chicken and bake for 20-25 minutes.
4 Serve chicken with pan-juices and a rocket salad.

Serves 4

ingredients

200g/7oz fresh ricotta
1 cup rocket, roughly chopped
1/4 cup/45g/1 1/2oz pine nuts, toasted
1/2 red capsicum (pepper), roasted
and finely chopped
freshly ground pepper and salt
4 chicken breasts (200g/7oz each),
with skin on
1 tablespoon butter
250mL/9fl oz chicken stock

duck
with vinegar

Method:

1 Heat oil in a frypan and cook duck, skin side down, over a low heat until skin is golden. Turn and cook on other side.
2 Add vinegar, black pepper to taste, cinnamon and blueberries. Cover and cook over a low heat for 15 minutes, or until duck is tender.
3 To prepare flowers, gradually sift flour into water and mix with a fork until batter is smooth. If necessary add more water. Pour 2.5cm/1in oil into a frypan and heat until very hot. Dip flowers into the batter and cook a few at a time in oil until golden.
4 To serve, arrange duck and flowers on serving plate and spoon blueberry sauce over duck.
Note: Blueberries are used in this recipe, but any other berry fruit may be substituted.
Serves 4

ingredients

2 tablespoons sunflower oil
4 duck breasts, with skin on
3 tablespoons balsamic vinegar
freshly ground black pepper
¼ teaspoon ground cinnamon
4 tablespoons fresh blueberries
Zucchini (courgette) flowers
90g/3oz flour
250 mL/8fl oz water
oil for cooking
12 zucchini (courgette) flowers

chicken marsala

chicken
marsala

ingredients

4 large chicken breast fillets, pounded
seasoned flour
30g/1oz butter
2 tablespoons olive oil
185mL/6fl oz dry Marsala
4 tablespoons chicken stock
30g/1oz butter, softened
freshly ground black pepper

Method:

1 Coat chicken in flour and shake off excess. Heat butter and oil in a frypan, until butter is foaming. Add chicken and cook for 3 minutes each side.
2 Stir in Marsala, bring to the boil and simmer for 15 minutes, or until chicken is cooked. Remove chicken and set aside to keep warm. Add stock, bring to the boil and cook for 2 minutes. Whisk in softened butter and season to taste with black pepper. To serve, spoon sauce over chicken.
Serves 4

quail with rice
and olives

Method:

1 *Heat oil and butter in a frypan and cook onions and garlic over a low heat for 3 minutes, or until onions soften.*

2 *Add quail to pan and cook over a high heat until brown on all sides. Add sage, rosemary and black pepper to taste.*

3 *Stir in Marsala, bring to the boil and simmer for 20 minutes or until quail is cooked.*

4 *To prepare rice, place rice, butter, mortadella and olives in a saucepan and heat gently, stirring, until butter is melted. Mix in Parmesan cheese and basil. To serve, arrange rice on serving plate, top with quail and spoon a little of the pan juices over.*

Serves 4

ingredients

1 tablespoon olive oil
30g/1oz butter
2 onions, chopped
2 cloves garlic, crushed
8 quail, cleaned
5 fresh sage leaves
3 teaspoons chopped fresh rosemary
freshly ground black pepper
300mL/9¹/₂fl oz dry Marsala
<u>Olive rice</u>
375g/12oz rice, cooked
60g/2oz butter, chopped
6 slices mortadella, chopped
90g/3oz pitted black olives, chopped
3 tablespoons grated
fresh Parmesan cheese
3 tablespoons chopped fresh basil

tuna in piquant tomato sauce

seafood

Italy is surrounded on most sides by sea,

and you'll be surrounded on all sides by people clamouring for more of these tasty, easy Italian seafood dishes!

garlic
and rosemary mackerel

Method:

1 Heat oil and butter in a large frypan and cook garlic for 1 minute. Add cutlets and cook for 3-4 minutes each side or until browned.

2 Pour lemon juice over and sprinkle with rosemary. Season to taste with black pepper. Cover and simmer for 5-8 minutes or until flesh flakes when tested with a fork.

ingredients

1 tablespoon olive oil
30g/1oz butter
2 cloves garlic, crushed
4 large mackeral cutlets, or thick fillets
3 tablespoons lemon juice
2 teaspoons fresh rosemary, 1/2 teaspoon
dry rosemary leaves
freshly ground black pepper

spicy scallops
and mushrooms

Method:

1 Melt butter in a large frypan and cook mushrooms, spring onions (shallots) and garlic for 4-5 minutes. Remove from pan and set aside. Add scallops to pan and cook for 2-3 minutes or until tender. Remove from pan and set aside.

2 Stir in wine, chilli and parsley and cook over a high heat until reduced by half. Return mushroom mixture and scallops to pan, toss to combine.

Note: Scallops, mushrooms and garlic are a wonderful combination in this quick dish.

Serves 4

ingredients

45g/1¹/₂oz butter
500g/1 lb button mushrooms
6 spring onions (shallots), chopped
2 cloves garlic, crushed
500g/1 lb scallops, cleaned
60mL/2fl oz dry white wine
1 red chilli, seeded and finely sliced
3 tablespoons chopped fresh parsley

sardine
fritters

Method:

1 *Coat sardines in flour, dip in egg mixture, then coat with breadcrumbs.*
2 *To make minted chilli butter, place butter, mint, spring onions, garlic, pepper and chilli in a bowl and mix well. Place butter on a piece of plastic food wrap and roll into a log shape. Refrigerate until required.*
3 *Heat oil and one-third minted chilli butter in a large frypan and cook sardines for 1-2 minutes each side or until golden. Serve sardines topped with a slice of minted chilli butter.*

Serves 4

ingredients

12 fresh sardine filets
4 tablespoons plain flour
1 egg, blended with 2 tablespoons milk
125g dried breadcrumbs
oil for cooking
125g/4oz butter, softened
3 tablespoons finely chopped fresh mint
2 spring onions, finely chopped
1 clove garlic, crushed
1/4 teaspoon chopped red chilli
freshly ground black pepper

Oven temperature 180°C, 350°F, Gas 4

tuna
in piquant tomato sauce

Method:

1 Heat oil in a frypan and cook tuna for 2-3 minutes each side. Transfer to an ovenproof dish and reserve juices.

2 To make sauce, cook onion and garlic in pan for 4-5 minutes or until tender. Add reserved pan juices, tomatoes, tomato juice, capers, anchovies and oregano. Season to taste with black pepper. Bring to the boil and pour over tuna. Cover and bake at 180°C/350°F/Gas 4 for 20-30 minutes, or until tuna flakes when tested.

Serves 4

ingredients

1 tablespoon olive oil
4 fresh tuna cutlets
<u>Sauce</u>
1 onion, chopped
2 cloves garlic, crushed
440g/14oz canned Italian peeled tomatoes, undrained and mashed
125mL/4fl oz tomato juice
2 tablespoons capers, chopped
4 anchovy fillets, chopped
1/2 teaspoon dried oregano
freshly ground black pepper

lemony
prawn kebabs

Method:

1 To make marinade, place oil, lemon juice, garlic, chilli and sage in a bowl. Season to taste with black pepper and mix to combine. Add prawns and mushrooms and toss to coat with marinade. Set aside to marinate for 1 hour.

2 Thread prawns, mushrooms and green capsicum (peppers) alternately onto eight oiled wooden skewers. Grill kebabs for 8-10 minutes or until cooked, turning and basting with marinade during cooking.

Note: These are delightful on the barbecue.

Serves 4

ingredients

750g/1 ½ lb large uncooked prawns, peeled and deveined
16 button mushrooms, stalks removed
2 green capsicums (peppers), seeded and cut into 16 pieces
Marinade
60mL/2fl oz olive oil
2 tablespoons lemon juice
2 cloves garlic, crushed
1 small red chilli, seeded and finely chopped
1 tablespoon chopped fresh sage
freshly ground black pepper

cheesy
stuffed squid

Method:

1 To make stuffing, combine breadcrumbs, parsley, ricotta cheese, Parmesan cheese, oregano, garlic, cayenne and egg. Divide mixture into four equal portions and spoon into squid hoods. Secure ends with a toothpick or skewer.

2 Heat oil in a frypan and cook squid for 3-4 minutes each side or until brown. Add garlic, tomatoes, rosemary, wine, sugar and black pepper to taste. Reduce heat and simmer for 20-30 minutes or until squid is tender. To serve, remove skewers, slice squid and accompany with sauce.

Serves 4

ingredients

4 small squid hoods, cleaned
2 tablespoons olive oil
I clove garlic, crushed
440g/14oz canned Italian peeled
tomatoes, undrained and mashed
$1/2$ teaspoon dried rosemary
60mL/2fl oz dry white wine
$1/2$ teaspoon sugar
freshly ground black pepper
Stuffing
45g/1$1/2$oz breadcrumbs,
made from stale bread
4 tablespoons chopped fresh parsley
125g/4oz ricotta cheese
3 tablespoons/60g/2oz Parmesan cheese
$1/2$ teaspoon dried oregano
I clove garlic, crushed
pinch cayenne pepper
I egg, lightly beaten

chargrilled lamb with mint pesto
and creamy potatoes

meat

Italian cuisine has an extraordinary

number of different ways of cooking meat.
Italian cooks use herbs and spices to bring
out and enhance the flavour of the meat.

rack of veal
with thyme on roasted garlic mashed potato

Photograph opposite

rack of veal with thyme on roasted garlic mashed potato

ingredients

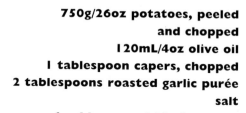

750g/26oz potatoes, peeled
and chopped
120mL/4oz olive oil
1 tablespoon capers, chopped
2 tablespoons roasted garlic purée
salt
freshly ground black pepper
2 tablespoons olive oil
1kg/2pt rack of veal (8 points)
2 tablespoons thyme leaves
300mL/10fl oz white wine
300mL/10fl oz veal or chicken stock

Method:

1 Preheat the oven to 180°C/350°F/Gas 4.
2 Boil the potatoes until soft. Drain, then mash (or purée), and add the olive oil, chopped capers and half the roasted garlic. Mix well, season with salt and pepper (to taste), and set aside until ready to serve.
3 Heat olive oil in a pan, and brown the veal on both sides until well sealed. This will take approximately 5 minutes. Remove the veal from the pan, and place on a rack in a baking dish. Rub the veal with remaining roasted garlic and 1 tablespoon of thyme leaves. Season with salt and pepper, add half the wine and stock to the baking dish.

4 Roast in the oven for 20 minutes or until veal is cooked to your liking. Wrap in foil and let rest for 10 minutes.
5 Add remaining stock, wine and thyme to the pan-juices and cook over a medium heat for 5 minutes or until the liquid has reduced by a third.
6 Serve the veal on a bed of mashed potatoes with pan-juices and sage leaves.

Serves 4

osso bucco

Method:

1 Melt butter in a frypan and cook carrot, onions, celery and garlic gently for 5 minutes, or until vegetables are softened. Remove vegetables from pan and place in an ovenproof dish.

2 Coat veal in flour. Heat oil in a frypan and cook veal until golden on each side. Remove from pan and arrange over vegetables.

3 Add tomatoes and cook, stirring constantly, for 5 minutes. Blend in wine, stock, bay leaf and black pepper to taste, bring to the boil and simmer for 5 minutes. Whisk in butter mixture and pour over meat and vegetables.

4 Cover dish and bake at 180°C/350°F/Gas 4 for 1½ hours or until meat is tender.

5 To make Gremolata, combine parsley, lemon rind, garlic and anchovy. Sprinkle over meat just prior to serving.

Note: Luxurious slow baking, intriguing stuffings and the use of unusual cuts characterise the cooking of most meats in Italy. Learn the secrets: the name of this recipe means 'hollow bones' and is a specialty from Milan.

Serves 4

ingredients

30g/1oz butter
1 carrot, chopped
2 onions, chopped
2 stalks celery, chopped
2 cloves garlic, crushed
4 thick slices shin veal on the bone
flour
2 tablespoons olive oil
8 tomatoes, peeled and chopped
125mL/4fl oz dry white wine
250mL/8fl oz beef stock
1 bay leaf
freshly ground black pepper
1 tablespoon butter mixed with
2 tablespoons flour
<u>Gremolata</u>
4 tablespoons fresh parsley, chopped
1 tablespoon lemon rind, finely grated
1 clove garlic, crushed
1 anchovy, finely chopped

Oven temperature 180°C, 350°F, Gas 4

chargrilled
lamb with mint pesto and creamy potatoes

Method:

1 *Preheat oven to 180°C/350°F/Gas 4. Season lamb with salt and freshly ground pepper to taste and set aside.*

2 *Lightly grease an ovenproof dish with butter and arrange the potato slices in overlapping rows in the dish, seasoning between each layer with salt and pepper, garlic and nutmeg.*

3 *Mix the flour and Parmesan cheese into the cream and pour over the potatoes. Sprinkle with extra Parmesan cheese then bake in the oven for 40-45 minutes or until potatoes are cooked.*

4 *To make the pesto: place the mint, parsley, garlic, pine nuts and cheeses in the bowl of a food processor, and process until finely chopped. Add the olive oil in a steady stream with the processor still running. Season with salt and pepper then set aside.*

5 *Preheat the chargrill plate (or pan), and grease lightly with a little oil. Chargrill the lamb on both sides for approximately 5-10 minutes or until done to your liking.*

6 *Serve the lamb sliced diagonally, on a bed of creamy potatoes with the mint pesto.*

Serves 4-6

ingredients

4 lamb backstraps (450g/1 lb in total)
salt and freshly ground black pepper
Creamy potatoes
500g/1 lb potatoes, thinly sliced
salt and freshly ground black pepper
1 garlic clove, crushed
1 teaspoon nutmeg
1 tablespoon plain flour
¹/₃ cup/40g/1¹/₃oz Parmesan cheese, grated
1 cup/250mL/8fl oz cream
2 tablespoons Parmesan cheese, grated (extra)
Mint pesto
1 cup/60g/2oz mint leaves
¹/₂ cup/30g/1oz parsley leaves
2 cloves garlic
¹/₂ cup/90g/3oz pine nuts, toasted
3 tablespoons Parmesan cheese, grated
3 tablespoons pecorino cheese, grated
¹/₃ cup/85mL/2¹/₂fl oz olive oil

Oven temperature 180°C, 350°F, Gas 4

seared beef
with mushrooms and garlic

Method:

1 *Soak the porcini mushrooms in boiling water for 20 minutes. Drain and chop. Set aside.*
2 *Heat the oil in a shallow pan, and cook the beef for a few minutes on each side. Remove from pan. Sauté the onion and the garlic (for a few minutes), then add all of the mushrooms and cook over high heat (until they are soft).*
3 *Add the wine and stock, bring to the boil, and then simmer for 10 minutes. Remove from the heat, add the parsley and season with salt and pepper.*
4 *Serve the beef with the mushrooms and sprinkle with extra chopped parsley.*

ingredients

50g/1³/₄oz dried porcini mushrooms
60mL/2fl oz olive oil
**1.2kg/2¹/₂ lb rump or fillet steak
(cut into 6 steaks)**
1 brown onion, chopped
2 garlic cloves, crushed
350g/12oz shiitake/button mushrooms
60mL/2fl oz red wine
250mL/9fl oz brown stock
2 tablespoons parsley, chopped
salt and pepper
parsley, chopped (extra)

Serves 6

Method:

1 Heat butter and oil in a large saucepan. When butter is foaming, add pork and brown on all sides.

2 Add milk, pepper to taste and bring to the boil. Reduce heat to low, cover and cook for 1½-2 hours or until pork is cooked. Brush pork occasionally with milk during cooking.

3 At end of cooking time, milk should have coagulated and browned in bottom of pan. If this has not occurred remove lid, and bring, liquid to the boil and boil until brown.

4 Remove meat from pan and set aside to cool slightly. Remove string from pork, cut into slices and arrange on a serving platter. Set aside to keep warm.

5 Remove any fat from pan, stir in water and bring to the boil, scraping residue from base of the pan. Strain and spoon pan juices over pork to serve.

Note: This dish originates from Bologna and is often preceded by dishes with a Bolognese sauce. Pork cooked this way also goes well with artichokes.

Serves 4

pork
braised in milk

ingredients

**30g/1oz butter
1 tablespoon vegetable oil
1kg/2 lb boneless loin pork,
rolled and tied
500mL/16fl oz milk
freshly ground black pepper
3 tablespoons warm water**

lamb shanks
with root vegetables

Method:

1 Heat half the oil in a large heavy-based saucepan, add root vegetables and onions and cook quickly until brown. Set aside on a plate. Add remaining oil to pan and brown the garlic and shanks for a few minutes.

2 Add the stock, water, red wine, tomato paste, rosemary, bouquet garni, pepper and salt to the pan. Bring to the boil, reduce the heat, and leave to simmer with the lid on for 20 minutes.

3 Return the vegetables to the pan and continue to cook for another 30 minutes until vegetables and lamb are cooked.

4 Before serving, remove the bouquet garni and adjust the seasoning to taste.

Serves 4

ingredients

40mL/1¹/₂fl oz olive oil
2 parsnips, peeled, and cut into large chunks
1 medium kumera, peeled, cut into large chunks
1 swede, peeled, and cut into large chunks
1 bunch spring onions, trimmed
2 cloves garlic, crushed
4 lamb shanks
200mL/7fl oz beef stock
65mL/2¹/₄fl oz water
125mL/4¹/₂fl oz red wine
1 tablespoon tomato paste
2 sprigs rosemary, chopped
bouquet garni
salt and freshly ground pepper

garlic
veal steaks

Method:

1 Heat half the oil in a nonstick frying pan over a low heat. Add garlic and cook, stirring, until golden and soft. Remove garlic from pan and set aside.

2 Increase heat to high, add veal, lemon rind and thyme and cook veal for 1-1½ minutes each side. Remove steaks from pan, top with garlic, set aside and keep warm.

3 Heat remaining oil in frying pan over a high heat, add eggplant (aubergine) and stir-fry for 3 minutes. Add wine, tomatoes and basil and stir-fry for 3 minutes longer or until eggplant (aubergine) is tender. Season to taste with black pepper.

4 To serve, arrange veal, garlic and eggplant (aubergine) mixture on serving plates and serve immediately.

Note: This dish is also delicious made with lamb steaks or chops instead of veal.

Serves 4

ingredients

1 tablespoon vegetable oil
6 cloves garlic
4 veal steaks or chops
2 teaspoons finely grated lemon rind
1 tablespoon chopped fresh thyme or
1 teaspoon dried thyme
1 eggplant (aubergine), cut into matchsticks
¼ cup/60mL/2fl oz red wine
2 tomatoes, chopped
1 tablespoon chopped fresh basil
freshly ground black pepper

sausage and roast capsicum
(pepper) salad

salads

In Italy, vegetables are often ordered

*as separate side dishes, and much importance
is attached to their taste and appearance.
Salads are also being treated with growing
reverence and innovation.*

artichoke
salad with pesto dressing

Method:
1 *Break watercress into small pieces and place in a bowl. Arrange artichokes, tomatoes and bocconcini cheese over watercress.*
2 *To make dressing, place basil, oil, garlic, Parmesan cheese and pine nuts in a food processor or blender and process until smooth. Drizzle over salad and toss gently to coat salad ingredients.*

ingredients

1 bunch watercress, washed
410 g/13 oz canned artichoke hearts, drained
4 tomatoes, peeled and diced
2 bocconcini cheese, sliced

Pesto dressing
60 g/2 oz fresh basil leaves
3 tablespoons olive oil
1 clove garlic, crushed
3 tablespoons grated fresh Parmesan cheese
2 tablespoons pine nuts, toasted

marinated
mushroom salad

Method:
1 *Whisk together basil, parsley, garlic, lemon juice, red and white wine vinegars and oil.*
2 *Place red capsicums (peppers) and mushrooms in a bowl. Pour over dressing. Toss. Cover. Marinate in the refrigerator for 3 hours.*

ingredients

8 roasted red capsicums (peppers), skinned and cut into thick strips
125g/4oz mushrooms, sliced

Herb and garlic dressing
1 tablespoon chopped basil
1 tablespoon chopped parsley
2 cloves garlic, crushed
2 tablespoons lemon juice
2 tablespoons red wine vinegar
2 tablespoons white wine vinegar
2 tablespoons safflower oil

spiral
pasta salad

Method:

1 Cook pasta in boiling water in a large saucepan following packet directions. Drain, rinse under cold running water and set aside to cool completely.

2 Place pasta, sun-dried tomatoes, artichokes, sun-dried or roasted capsicums (peppers), olives, basil, Parmesan cheese, oil and vinegar in a bowl and toss to combine. Cover and refrigerate for 2 hours or until ready to serve.

Note: A wonderful salad that combines all the best flavours of Italy. It is delicious served with crusty bread and baked ricotta cheese. If you can, make it a day in advance so that the flavours have time to develop.

Serves 4

ingredients

500g/1 lb spiral pasta
100g/3¹/₂oz sun-dried tomatoes, thinly sliced
100g/3¹/₂oz marinated artichoke hearts, chopped
75g/2¹/₂oz sun-dried or roasted capsicums (peppers), chopped
125g/4oz marinated black olives
12 small fresh basil leaves
60g/2oz Parmesan cheese shavings
1 tablespoon olive oil
3 tablespoons balsamic or red wine vinegar

sausage
and roast capsicum (pepper) salad

Photograph opposite

ingredients

125g/4oz penne, cooked and cooled
2 red capsicums (peppers), roasted and cut into strips
2 yellow or green capsicums (peppers), roasted and cut into strips
125g/4oz button mushrooms, sliced
155g/5oz pitted black olives
5 English spinach leaves, stalks removed and leaves finely chopped

Herbed beef sausages
500g/1 lb lean beef mince
185g/6oz sausage meat
2 cloves garlic, crushed
1 teaspoon chopped fresh rosemary
1 tablespoon finely chopped fresh basil
2 slices proscuitto or lean ham, finely chopped
1 tablespoon olive oil
freshly ground black pepper

Herb dressing
1/2 cup/125mL/4fl oz olive oil
1/4 cup/60mL/2fl oz balsamic or red wine vinegar
2 teaspoons chopped fresh basil or 1 teaspoon dried basil
1 teaspoon chopped fresh oregano or 1/4 teaspoon dried oregano
freshly ground black pepper

sausage and roast capsicum (pepper) salad

Method:

1 To make sausages, place beef, sausage meat, garlic, rosemary, basil, proscuitto or ham, olive oil and black pepper to taste in a bowl and mix to combine. Shape mixture into 10 cm/ 4in long sausages. Cook sausages under a preheated medium grill, turning occasionally, for 10-15 minutes or until brown and cooked through. Set aside to cool slightly, then cut each sausage into diagonal slices.

2 To make dressing, place olive oil, vinegar, basil, oregano and black pepper to taste in a screwtop jar and shake well to combine.

3 Place sausage slices, penne, red yellow or green capsicums (peppers), mushrooms and olives in bowl, spoon over dressing and toss to combine. Line a serving platter with spinach leaves, then top with sausage and vegetable mixture.

Note: To prevent pasta that is for use in a salad from sticking together, rinse it under cold running water immediately after draining. All this mouth-watering salad needs to make a complete meal is some crusty bread or wholemeal rolls.

Serves 4

65

spicy asparagus
with pine nuts

Method:

1 *Steam or microwave asparagus until just tender. Drain and rinse under cold running water to refresh, then drain again and set aside.*

2 *Heat butter in a frypan and cook pine nuts and salami until lightly browned. Add asparagus and basil and cook, stirring constantly, for 1 minute or until heated through. Sprinkle with Parmesan cheese and serve immediately.*

Note: *This recipe makes a delicious entrée. Use bacon instead of salami for a less spicy flavour.*

Serves 4

ingredients

**500g/1 lb fresh asparagus spears, trimmed
and cut into 5cm/2in pieces
15g/¹/₂oz butter
60g/2oz pine nuts
125g/4oz hot Italian salami,
cut into 5mm/¹/₄in cubes
2 tablespoons fresh basil, chopped
3 tablespoons fresh Parmesan cheese, grated**

radicchio anchovy salad

radicchio
anchovy salad

Method:

1 *Arrange radicchio, endive and witloof (chicory) attractively on a large platter. Top with radishes and parsley.*

2 *To make dressing, place oil, lemon juice, wine, anchovies, garlic and sugar in a food processor or blender and process until smooth. Drizzle dressing over salad just before serving.*

Serves 6

ingredients

**1 radicchio lettuce, washed
and leaves separated
¹/₂ bunch curly endive,
washed and leaves separated
1 witloof (chicory),
washed and leaves separated
8 radishes, washed and sliced
3 tablespoons chopped fresh
Italian flat-leaf parsley
Dressing
60mL/2fl oz olive oil
60mL/2fl oz lemon juice
60mL/2fl oz dry white wine
2 cloves garlic, crushed
3 anchovy fillets, drained and chopped
¹/₂ teaspoon sugar**

fennel
and orange salad

Method:
1 *Place endive on a large serving platter. Arrange fennel, oranges, onion and olives attractively over endive.*
2 *To make dressing, place oil, vinegar, fennel leaves, orange rind, sugar and black pepper to taste in a screw-top jar. Shake well to combine. Pour dressing over salad and serve immediately.*

Serves 6

ingredients

**1 bunch curly endive,
leaves separated and washed
1 small fennel bulb, cut into thin strips
3 oranges, peeled and segmented
1 onion, sliced
20 black olives
<u>Orange dressing</u>
3 1/2 tablespoons olive oil
3 tablespoons white wine vinegar
1 tablespoon chopped fresh fennel leaves
1/2 teaspoon grated orange rind
1/2 teaspoon sugar
freshly ground black pepper**

cassata siciliana

desserts

When you see what treats are in

store for dessert, you might just decide to serve nothing but these creamy, sugary, crunchy, divinely indulgent delights. La dolce vita!

lemon
and basil granita

Method:

1 Combine basil, sugar and wine in a saucepan over medium heat. Bring to the boil. Cook, stirring, for 3 minutes.

2 Strain mixture. Discard solids. Cool to room temperature. Stir in lemon and lime juices and lemon rind.

3 Pour mixture into a shallow freezerproof container. Freeze until ice crystals start to form around the edges. Using a fork, stir to break up ice crystals. Repeat the process once more. Transfer mixture to ice cube trays. Freeze until firm.

ingredients

30g/1oz basil leaves, chopped
¼ cup/60g/2oz castor sugar
2 cups/500ml/16fl oz sweet white wine
1 cup/250ml/8fl oz lemon juice
¼ cup/60ml/2fl oz lime juice
1 tablespoon grated lemon rind

70

tiramisu

Method:

1 Place mascarpone, cream, brandy and sugar in a bowl, mix to combine and set aside. Dissolve coffee powder in boiling water and set aside.

2 Line the base of a 20 cm/8 in square dish with one-third of the sponge fingers. Sprinkle one-third of the coffee mixture over sponge fingers, then top with one-third of the mascarpone mixture. Repeat layers finishing with a layer of mascarpone mixture, sprinkle with grated chocolate and chill for 15 minutes before serving.

Note: Mascarpone is a fresh cheese made from cream. It is available from delicatessens and some supermarkets. If unavailable, mix one part sour cream with three parts lightly whipped cream (double) and use in its place.

Serves 4

ingredients

250g/8oz mascarpone
¹/₂ cup/125mL/8fl oz cream (double)
2 tablespoons brandy
¹/₄ cup/60g/2oz sugar
2 tablespoons instant coffee powder
1¹/₂ cups/375mL/12fl oz boiling water
1 x 250g/8oz packet sponge fingers
250g/8oz grated chocolate

cassata
siciliana

ingredients

Method:

1 Beat ricotta and sugar together until light and fluffy. Divide mixture in half. Fold pistachios and fruit through one half of mixture. Mix cinnamon, chocolate and Amaretto into other half. Cover and set aside.

2 Line base and sides of a 20cm/8in bowl or mould with plastic foodwrap, then with three-quarters of the cake slices. Fill with ricotta mixture and cover with remaining cake slices. Cover and freeze for 2 hours.

3 When mixture is set, pour chocolate mixture over it, return to freezer until set.

4 To make topping, whip cream and Amaretto together until soft peaks form. Just prior to serving, turn out cassata, spread completely with cream and decorate with glacé fruit.

Note: This is a simple do-ahead dinner party dessert that looks spectacular when decorated with extra glacé fruit. It is best prepared a day before serving.

500g/1 lb ricotta cheese
250g/8oz sugar
2 tablespoons chopped pistachios
3 tablespoons chopped glacé fruit
1/4 teaspoon ground cinnamon
60g/2oz dark chocolate, grated
2 tablespoons Amaretto liqueur
20cm/8in-round sponge cake,
cut into 1cm/1/2in slices
Topping
250mL/8fl oz pure (single) cream
1 tablespoon Amaretto liqueur
a selection of glacé fruit

Serves 8

fig
and mascarpone cake

Method:

1 To make custard, place custard powder, sugar, milk, cream and vanilla essence in a saucepan and whisk until mixture is smooth. Cook over a low heat, stirring constantly, until custard thickens. Remove pan from heat and set aside to cool. Fold mascarpone into cooled custard and set aside.

2 Line a 23cm/9in springform tin with nonstick baking paper and line the base with half the sponge fingers. Sprinkle with half the marsala, top with half the sliced figs and half the custard. Repeat layers to use all ingredients. Cover with plastic food wrap and refrigerate for 4 hours or until cake has set.

3 Remove cake from tin. Decorate the top with extra figs.

Note: When figs are not in season, fresh strawberries make a suitable substitute for this elegant charlotte.

Makes a 23cm/9in round cake

ingredients

32 sponge fingers
¹/₂ cup/125mL/4fl oz marsala
or sweet sherry
6 fresh figs, sliced
extra figs to decorate

Mascarpone custard
3 tablespoons custard powder
2 tablespoons caster sugar
1 cup/250mL/8fl oz milk
1 cup/250mL/8fl oz cream (double)
1 teaspoon vanilla essence
375g/12oz mascarpone

Basic pizza dough

ingredients

**1 3/4 teaspoons active dry yeast,
or 15g/1/2oz fresh yeast, crumbled
pinch sugar
335mL/10 1/2fl oz warm water
125mL/4fl oz olive oil
500g/1 lb plain flour, sifted
1 1/4 teaspoons salt**

1 Dissolve yeast and sugar in water in a large mixing bowl. Set aside in a draught-free place for 5 minutes or until foamy. Stir in oil, flour and salt and mix until a rough dough forms. Turn out onto a lightly floured surface and knead for 5 minutes or until soft and satiny. Add more flour if necessary.
2 Lightly oil a large bowl then roll dough around in it to cover surface with oil. Seal bowl with plastic foodwrap and place in a warm, draught-free spot for 1 1/2-2 hours or until dough has doubled in volume.
3 Knock down and remove dough from bowl. Knead briefly before rolling out on a floured surface to desired shape. If dough feels too stiff, set aside to rest for a few minutes and start again.
4 Transfer to an oiled pizza pan and finish shaping by hand, forming a slightly raised rim. The dough should be approximately 5mm/1/4in thick. For a thicker crust, cover with a clean tea-towel and set aside for 30 minutes to rise again. The pizza is now ready for topping and baking.

To make in a food processor:
Dissolve yeast and sugar in water in a small bowl. Set aside for 5 minutes or until foamy. Put flour and salt in food processor and pulse once or twice to sift. With machine running, slowly pour in yeast mixture and process for 10-15 seconds longer. Transfer to a lightly floured surface and knead by hand for 3-4 minutes. Continue as for basic recipe.

**Dough for a 38-40cm/
15-16in-round pizza**

Focaccia dough

ingredients

**1 1/4 teaspoons active dry yeast
1 teaspoon sugar
315mL/9 1/2fl oz lukewarm water
1 tablespoon olive oil
500g/1 lb plain flour, sifted**

1 Place yeast and sugar in a large bowl and stir in all but 1 tablespoon water. Cover and set aside in a warm place for 8-10 minutes or until foaming.
2 Stir in remaining water and oil. Add one-third flour and stir until smooth. Stir in the next one-third flour, beat, then add remaining flour. Mix until a rough dough forms. Transfer to a floured board and knead for 8-10 minutes, or until dough is smooth and satiny.
3 Place dough in a lightly oiled bowl; roll around to coat dough with oil. Cover bowl tightly with plastic foodwrap. Set aside in a warm, draught-free spot for 1 1/2 hours or until doubled in size.
4 Knock dough down, knead once or twice, then roll to desired shape. Place on an oiled oven tray, brush surface with a little oil, cover with a clean tea-towel and set aside to rise for 30 minutes longer.
5 Using your fingertips, dimple entire surface of dough, pushing in about halfway. Traditionally this serves to create little pools for the olive oil, but it also kneads the dough one last time. Re-cover with tea-towel and set aside again to rise for 1 1/2-2 hours or until doubled. The focaccia is now ready for dressing and baking.

To make in a food processor:
In a small bowl, stir yeast and sugar into warm water, cover and set aside in a warm place for 8-10 minutes or until foamy. Put flour and salt in processor bowl and pulse 2 or 3 times to mix. With machine running, pour in additional water, yeast and oil. Process until a rough dough forms, then continue to process to knead dough into a firm ball. Transfer to a floured board and knead by hand for 2-3 minutes.

**Dough for a 28x38cm/
11x15in focaccia**

breads

Spinach, olive and onion bread

ingredients

1 recipe Focaccia Dough, (page 74)
1 tablespoon olive oil
1 egg white, lightly beaten
Filling
2 tablespoons olive oil
1 large red onion, sliced
1 clove garlic, crushed
1 tablespoon sultanas
**750g/1½ lb spinach, stalks removed
and leaves shredded**
125g/4oz stuffed green olives, sliced
**3 tablespoons fresh mozzarella
cheese, grated**
freshly ground black pepper

1 *Prepare Focaccia Dough, as described in recipe through to end of Step 3.*
2 *To make filling, heat olive oil in a large frypan and cook onion until soft. Add garlic and sultanas and cook 1 minute longer.*

Add spinach and olives and cook over a medium heat until spinach just begins to wilt. Remove from heat and mix in mozzarella. Season to taste with black pepper. Set aside.
3 *Knock down dough and knead lightly. Divide dough into four portions, and roll each out into 5mm/¼in-thick circles. Place two circles on lightly oiled baking trays, then spread filling to within 2.5cm/1in of edge. Cover with remaining circles and pinch sides together to seal edges.*
4 *Brush top with olive oil. Cover with a clean tea-towel and set aside to rise in a warm place until doubled in size.*
5 *Brush top with egg white and bake at 200°C/ 400°F/Gas 6 for 25 minutes, or until golden brown and well risen.*
Note: *A filled bread, almost a pie, this flat loaf makes a delicious snack or supper dish.*
Serves 8

pizzas

Artichoke, mozzarella and salami pizza

ingredients

¹/₂ recipe Basic Pizza Dough (page 74)
olive oil
300g/9¹/₂oz fresh mozzarella,
thinly sliced
100g/3¹/₂oz Milano salami, thinly sliced
4 canned artichoke hearts, thinly
sliced lengthways
freshly ground black pepper

1 *Roll dough into rectangle 1cm/¹/₂in thick and press into a lightly oiled, shallow 28x18cm/ 11x7in tin and bring dough up at edges to form a slight rim. Brush with olive oil.*
2 *Place slices of mozzarella, slices of salami and slices of artichoke heart slightly overlapping in lines along width of dough. Continue forming rows of mozzarella, salami and artichoke heart until surface is covered. Sprinkle generously with olive oil, and season to taste with black pepper.*
3 *Bake at 220°C/425°F for 15 minutes, then reduce heat to 190°C/375°F and bake for 10 minutes longer or until cheese is bubbling and crust golden brown. Remove from oven and rest briefly before serving.*
    Note: *Not all pizzas need a layer of tomato sauce to give them flavour and keep them moist. This tasty combination of toppings is a delicious and striking example.*
    Makes 1 pizza

Pizza Supremo

ingredients

2 quantities Basic Pizza Dough (page 74)
³/₄ cup/185mL/6 fl oz tomato
paste (purée)
1 green capsicum (pepper), chopped
155g/5oz sliced peperoni or salami
155g/5oz ham or prosciutto, sliced
125g/4oz mushrooms, sliced
440g/14oz canned pineapple
pieces, drained
60g/2oz pitted olives
125g/4oz mozzarella cheese, grated
125g/4oz tasty cheese (mature
Cheddar), grated

1 *Prepare pizza dough as described in recipe. Divide dough into two portions and shape each to form a 30cm/12in round. Place rounds on lightly greased baking trays and spread with tomato paste (purée).*
2 *Arrange half the green capsicum(pepper), peperoni or salami, ham or prosciutto, mushrooms, pineapple and olives attractively on each pizza base.*
3 *Combine mozzarella cheese and tasty cheese (mature Cheddar) and sprinkle half the mixture over each pizza. Bake for 25-30 minutes or until cheese is golden and base is crisp.*
    Note: *If you only want to make one pizza, halve the topping ingredients and use only one quantity of dough. But remember everyone loves pizza and they always eat more than you – or they – think they will.*
    Serves 8

Cooking is not an exact science: one does not require finely calibrated scales, pipettes and scientific equipment to cook, yet the conversion to metric measures in some countries and its interpretations must have intimidated many a good cook.

Weights are given in the recipes only for ingredients such as meats, fish, poultry and some vegetables. Though a few grams/ounces one way or another will not affect the success of your dish.

Though recipes have been tested using the Australian Standard 250mL cup, 20mL tablespoon and 5mL teaspoon, they will work just as well with the US and Canadian 8fl oz cup, or the UK 300mL cup. We have used graduated cup measures in preference to tablespoon measures so that proportions are always the same. Where tablespoon measures have been given, these are not crucial measures, so using the smaller tablespoon of the US or UK will not affect the recipe's success. At least we all agree on the teaspoon size.

For breads, cakes and pastries, the only area which might cause concern is where eggs are used, as proportions will then vary. If working with a 250mL or 300mL cup, use large eggs (60g/2oz), adding a little more liquid to the recipe for 300mL cup measures if it seems necessary. Use the medium-sized eggs (55g/1¼oz) with 8fl oz cup measure. A graduated set of measuring cups and spoons is recommended, the cups in particular for measuring dry ingredients. Remember to level such ingredients to ensure their accuracy.

English measures

All measurements are similar to Australian with two exceptions: the English cup measures 300mL/10fl oz, whereas the Australian cup measure 250mL/8fl oz. The English tablespoon (the Australian dessertspoon) measures 14.8mL/¹/₂fl oz against the Australian tablespoon of 20mL/³/₄fl oz.

American measures

The American reputed pint is 16fl oz, a quart is equal to 32fl oz and the American gallon, 128fl oz. The Imperial measurement is 20fl oz to the pint, 40fl oz a quart and 160fl oz one gallon.

The American tablespoon is equal to 14.8mL/¹/₂fl oz, the teaspoon is 5mL/¹/₆fl oz. The cup measure is 250mL/8fl oz, the same as Australia.

Dry measures

All the measures are level, so when you have filled a cup or spoon, level it off with the edge of a knife. The scale below is the "cook's equivalent"; it is not an exact conversion of metric to imperial measurement. To calculate the exact metric equivalent yourself, use 2.2046 lb = 1 kg or 1 lb = 0.45359kg

Metric		Imperial	
g = grams		oz = ounces	
kg = kilograms		lb = pound	
15g		¹/₂oz	
20g		²/₃oz	
30g		1oz	
60g		2oz	
90g		3oz	
125g		4oz	¹/₄ lb
155g		5oz	
185g		6oz	
220g		7oz	
250g		8oz	¹/₂ lb
280g		9oz	
315g		10oz	
345g		11oz	
375g		12oz	³/₄ lb
410g		13oz	
440g		14oz	
470g		15oz	
1,000g	1kg	35.2oz	2.2 lb
	1.5kg		3.3 lb

Oven temperatures

The Celsius temperatures given here are not exact; they have been rounded off and are given as a guide only. Follow the manufacturer's temperature guide, relating it to oven description given in the recipe. Remember gas ovens are hottest at the top, electric ovens at the bottom and convection-fan forced ovens are usually even throughout. We included Regulo numbers for gas cookers which may assist. To convert °C to °F multiply °C by 9 and divide by 5 then add 32.

Oven temperatures

	C°	F°	Regulo
Very slow	120	250	1
Slow	150	300	2
Moderately slow	150	325	3
Moderate	180	350	4
Moderately hot	190-200	370-400	5-6
Hot	210-220	410-440	6-7
Very hot	230	450	8
Super hot	250-290	475-500	9-10

Cake dish sizes

Metric	Imperial
15cm	6in
18cm	7in
20cm	8in
23cm	9in

Loaf dish sizes

Metric	Imperial
23x12cm	9x5in
25x8cm	10x3in
28x18cm	11x7in

Liquid measures

Metric	Imperial	Cup & Spoon
mL	fl oz	
millilitres	fluid ounce	
5mL	$1/6$fl oz	1 teaspoon
20mL	$2/3$fl oz	1 tablespoon
30mL	1fl oz	1 tablespoon plus 2 teaspoons
60mL	2fl oz	$1/4$ cup
85mL	$2^{1}/_{2}$fl oz	$1/3$ cup
100mL	3fl oz	$3/8$ cup
125mL	4fl oz	$1/2$ cup
150mL	5fl oz	$1/4$ pint, 1 gill
250mL	8fl oz	1 cup
300mL	10fl oz	$1/2$ pint)
360mL	12fl oz	$1^{1}/_{2}$ cups
420mL	14fl oz	$1^{3}/_{4}$ cups
500mL	16fl oz	2 cups
600mL	20fl oz 1 pint,	$2^{1}/_{2}$ cups
1 litre	35fl oz 1 $3/4$ pints,	4 cups

Cup measurements

One cup is equal to the following weights.

	Metric	Imperial
Almonds, flaked	90g	3oz
Almonds, slivered, ground	125g	4oz
Almonds, kernel	155g	5oz
Apples, dried, chopped	125g	4oz
Apricots, dried, chopped	190g	6oz
Breadcrumbs, packet	125g	4oz

	Metric	Imperial
Breadcrumbs, soft	60g	2oz
Cheese, grated	125g	4oz
Choc bits	155g	5oz
Coconut, desiccated	90g	3oz
Cornflakes	30g	1oz
Currants	155g	5oz
Flour	125g	4oz
Fruit, dried (mixed, sultanas etc)	185g	6oz
Ginger, crystallised, glace	250g	8oz
Honey, treacle, golden syrup	315g	10oz
Mixed peel	220g	7oz
Nuts, chopped	125g	4oz
Prunes, chopped	220g	7oz
Rice, cooked	155g	5oz
Rice, uncooked	220g	7oz
Rolled oats	90g	3oz
Sesame seeds	125g	4oz
Shortening (butter, margarine)	250g	8oz
Sugar, brown	155g	5oz
Sugar, granulated or caster	250g	8oz
Sugar, sifted icing	155g	5oz
Wheatgerm	60g	2oz

Length

Some of us still have trouble converting imperial length to metric. In this scale, measures have been rounded off to the easiest-to-use and most acceptable figures.

To obtain the exact metric equivalent in converting inches to centimetres, multiply inches by 2.54 whereby 1 inch equals 25.4 millimetres and 1 millimetre equals 0.03937 inches.

Metric	Imperial
mm=millimetres	in = inches
cm=centimetres	ft = feet
5mm, 0.5cm	$1/4$in
10mm, 1.0cm	$1/2$in
20mm, 2.0cm	$3/4$in
2.5cm	1in
5cm	2in
8cm	3in
10cm	4in
12cm	5in
15cm	6in
18cm	7in
20cm	8in
23cm	9in
25cm	10in
28cm	11in
30cm	1 ft, 12in

index